How to Draw the Life and Times of
John Quincy Adams

Betsy Dru Tecco

The Rosen Publishing Group's
PowerKids Press™
New York

To my politically minded mother, who loves history

Published in 2006 by The Rosen Publishing Group, Inc.
29 East 21st Street, New York, NY 10010

First Edition

Editors: Kara Murray and Rachel O'Connor
Layout Design: Elana Davidian

Illustrations: All illustrations by Albert Hanner.
Photo Credits: p. 4 United States Department of State Art Collection; p. 7 © North Wind Picture Archives; p. 8 © Corbis; p. 9 Courtesy of Quincy Historical Society, Quincy Massachusetts; p. 10 U.S. Dept. of the Interior, National Park Service, Adams National Historical Park; p. 12 © Gianni Dagli Orti/Corbis; p. 14 Picture History; p. 16 Prints and Drawings Collection, The Octagon, The Museum of The American Architectural Foundation, Washington DC. Photograph by Lee Stalsworth; p. 20 National Museum of American History, Smithsonian Institution, S64-62; p. 24 New Haven Colony Historical Society; p. 26 Library of Congress Prints and Photographs Division; p. 28 © Bettman/Corbis.

Library of Congress Cataloging-in-Publication Data

Tecco, Betsy Dru.
How to draw the life and times of John Quincy Adams / Betsy Dru Tecco.— 1st ed.
    p. cm. — (A kid's guide to drawing the presidents of the United States of America)
Includes bibliographical references and index.
ISBN 1-4042-2983-3 (lib. bdg.)
1. Adams, John Quincy, 1767–1848—Juvenile literature. 2. Presidents—United States—Biography—Juvenile literature. 3. Drawing—Technique—Juvenile literature. I. Title. II. Series.

E377.T43 2006
973.5'5'092—dc22

                                    2004015967

Manufactured in the United States of America

Contents

Young John Quincy Adams

John Quincy Adams was the sixth president of the United States. He was born on July 11, 1767, in Braintree, Massachusetts. He was the oldest son of John and Abigail Adams. John Adams was the second U.S. president. He signed the Declaration of Independence in  1776 and was an important leader in the American Revolution. Abigail Adams was one of the country's most admired first ladies. She named her oldest son after her grandfather, Colonel John Quincy, who died soon after John Quincy Adams was born.

Adams grew up during the American Revolution, in which the American colonies fought for freedom from British rule. Adams's father was often away in Philadelphia, Pennsylvania, as a member of the Continental Congress. Young Adams stayed on the family farm with his mother, older sister, and younger brothers. As the first son, John Quincy became responsible for many tasks in the household.

When he was only nine years old, Adams volunteered to help the colonists win the war for independence by carrying messages between Braintree and Boston. He rode the 10 miles (16 km) on horseback to deliver daily news between the two towns. Adams was brave to volunteer, because the British often captured messengers.

Throughout his life Adams worried about whether he was good enough. Instead of being pleased with a job well done, he would push himself to greater success. Even as a little boy, he promised his father that he would try to work more and play less. Adams grew up to become a highly accomplished man.

You will need the following supplies to draw the life and times of John Quincy Adams:

✓ A sketch pad   ✓ An eraser   ✓ A pencil   ✓ A ruler

These are some of the shapes and drawing terms you need to know:

Horizontal Line	——	Squiggly Line	
Oval		Trapezoid	
Rectangle		Triangle	
Shading		Vertical Line	
Slanted Line		Wavy Line	

A Life of Achievement

John Quincy Adams committed himself to a life of public service. He served first as an American ambassador. Then he became secretary of state under President James Monroe. Many people believe he was one of the best secretaries of state in the nation's history. The agreement he made with Spain in the Transcontinental Treaty of 1819 is considered to be one of the United States' greatest diplomatic triumphs. As a result of this treaty, for the first time one could travel from the Atlantic coast to the Pacific coast without leaving U.S. territory.

Adams became the sixth U.S. president in 1825. Unfortunately, he failed to accomplish all that he wanted to during his one term in office. He won the presidency in a very close election, and his rivals prevented him from completing many of his goals.

Adams was elected to the U.S. Congress in 1830. He is the only president to serve in the House of Representatives after his presidency. As a congressman, Adams fought hard against slavery.

John Quincy Adams is shown here addressing the House of Representatives during his time as a congressman following his presidency. Many people came to view him as a hero because he spoke out against slavery and stood up to the powerful southern congressmen.

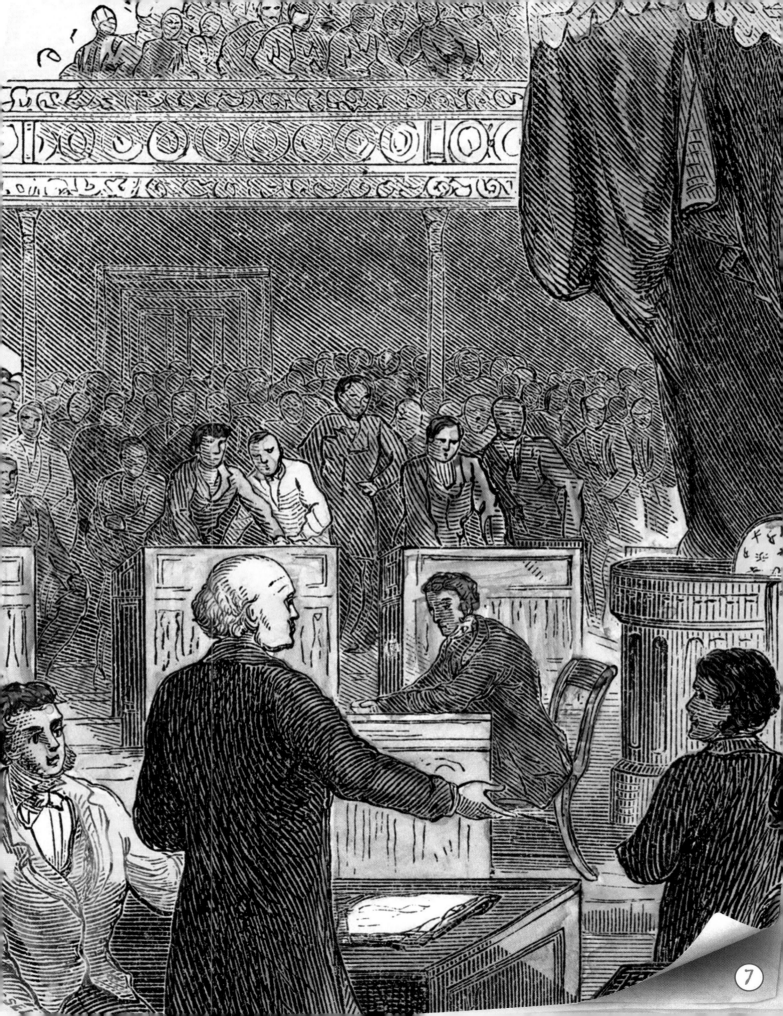

John Quincy Adams's Massachusetts

John Quincy Adams was born in the house on the right on July 11, 1767.

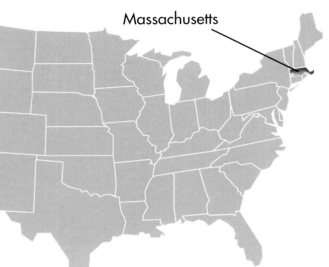

Massachusetts

Map of the United States of America

Massachusetts was one of the original 13 American colonies that had once belonged to Britain. It is also the birthplace of John Quincy Adams and the place where the American Revolution started. The war against the British began in 1775 with the Battle of Lexington and Concord in Massachusetts. Thirteen years later Massachusetts became the new nation's sixth state.

The Adams family lived on a farm in the town of Braintree, near Boston. In 1792, that part of Braintree was named Quincy in honor of Colonel John Quincy, the great-grandfather of John Quincy Adams. Today Quincy is often called the city of presidents because it was the birthplace of John

Adams, John Quincy Adams, and John Hancock, who was president of the Continental Congress from 1775 to 1777.

John Quincy Adams was born in the farmhouse next to the house where his father was born. Both houses can be found in the Adams National Historical Park. They are the oldest presidential birthplaces in the country that are still standing today. One mile (1.6 km) away is another house where Adams lived. His parents bought this house, known as the Old House, in 1787. Adams lived there from 1826 until his death in 1848. Nearby is the United First Parish Church, where both presidents and their wives are buried.

In a section of Quincy called Wollaston is Merrymount Park. The Adams family once owned this land. At the park's entrance is a bronze monument to John Adams and John Quincy Adams. It was made in 1926 by sculptor Bruce Wilder Saville to honor a father and son who committed their lives to aiding their country.

This monument in Merrymount Park in Quincy, Massachusetts, honors John Quincy Adams (right) and his father (left). Quincy is proud of these two great presidents.

Childhood Lessons

John Quincy Adams's parents wanted their oldest son to work in government someday, so they made sure that he received a good education. Adams never actually went to school in Quincy, but he studied with tutors and at home with his mother. Abigail Adams helped her son learn how to read and write. He loved books and studied the Bible regularly. Because his father was away so often when he was young, Adams began writing letters to him as early as age six. When he was 11 years old, Adams began writing about his daily experiences. He wrote in his private diary for nearly 70 years. Many people consider it the most valuable journal kept by any famous American.

In 1778, Adams traveled to Europe for the first time with his father, who was then a diplomat. It was a daring trip to make for a 10-year-old boy since the American Revolution was still going on. Abigail worried about her son's safety during the five-week trip.

1

Begin by drawing a rectangle. Now you are going to draw the statue of John Quincy Adams and his mother, Abigail. Abigail Adams taught her son and prepared him for success in life.

2

Draw the seven ovals, as shown, for her head, neck, arms, and torso. Position them carefully, using the drawing to help you. Draw the shape of her gown.

3

Draw 11 oval guides for young John Quincy Adams. Notice where some of the ovals overlap. Add the rounded shapes of his feet.

4

Begin adding the details on the figure of Abigail by outlining her head, hair, shoulders, arms, hands, and gown. Use the existing ovals to guide you in creating the shapes.

5

Now do the same for the figure of John Quincy Adams. Start with his head and work your way down. Don't forget to draw the outline of his jacket.

6

Erase the oval guides and any extra lines. Fill in the detail on the faces and the bodies. Draw the pen and paper in Abigail's hand and the book in John Quincy Adams's hand.

7

Add the lines for Abigail's hair, the folds in her cape and gown, and the last details on John Quincy Adams's head, shirt, coat, and shoes.

8

Erase the rectangle you drew in step 1. Finish with shading. You're done. Good work!

A Young Man of the World

When 10-year-old John Quincy Adams arrived in France, he attended Passy Academy in Paris. At age 14, he traveled to St. Petersburg, Russia, with Francis Dana, the first U.S. minister to Russia. He worked there for about one year as Dana's secretary. This  statue of Peter the Great in St. Petersburg was put up in 1782, the same year Adams lived in the city.

When he was 15, Adams traveled from St. Petersburg back to Paris. The journey took six months. Shortly after returning to Paris in 1783, Adams became his father's assistant during the negotiation of the Treaty of Paris. This treaty ended the American Revolution.

John Quincy Adams returned to Massachusetts in 1785 to study law at Harvard College. Adams graduated from Harvard with honors in 1787. For the next three years, he studied law under Judge Theophilus Parsons in Newburyport, Massachusetts.

1

You are now going to draw the statue of Peter the Great. Begin by drawing a rectangle.

2

Draw the outline of the rock base of the statue at the bottom of the rectangle. Draw a dotted line on the bottom and leave a small open space at the top.

3

Draw the outline shape of the horse and rider on top of the rock. See where the horse's back leg comes into the space you left on top of the rock.

4

Draw the outline within the guide shape you drew in step 3. Add details to the rider's face and draw his arm. Draw the horse's ears, eyes, mouth, and jaw.

5

Erase the guidelines. Add more details to the horse and rider. Start with the cape on the rider, then draw his legs and the saddle blanket. Next draw the horse's remaining legs. Draw part of the horse's rein.

6

Erase the rectangular guide that you drew in step 1. Then draw the fence around the base of the rock. First draw the curved lines circling the statue, then finish with the small vertical rectangles.

7

Draw the curved shape connecting the horse and the rock. Then add details to the horse, the rider, and the rock.

8

You can finish by shading your drawing. Notice how the shading is darker in some parts than others. Good work!

Marriage and Family

When John Quincy Adams was 28 years old, he was in London on business. There he met Louisa Catherine Johnson. Her father was an American diplomat in Britain. In 1797, they were married in London. That same year Adams's father was elected the second U.S.

president. He appointed his son American ambassador to Prussia, which was then part of Germany. For the next four years, John Quincy and Louisa Adams lived in Berlin.

Over the course of their 50-year marriage, the Adamses lived in Massachusetts, Russia, London, and Washington, D.C. Louisa and John Quincy had three sons and one daughter, who died as a baby. Their firstborn son, named George Washington after the first U.S. president, died at age 28 in an accident. Their second son, John Adams II, died suddenly in 1834 at the age of 31. Their third son, Charles Francis, became an American diplomat and a congressman.

1

You are now going to draw Louisa Adams. Begin by drawing a square.

2

Draw one circle and two ovals. First draw the oval on top. This is for the head. Next draw the circle for the body. Draw the oval for her neck. Make sure it connects the circle to the top oval.

3

Draw another circle. This is your guide for her shoulder. Draw a small circle on the left with a squiggly line coming from the bottom. Draw the guide for her shoulder and arm on the right.

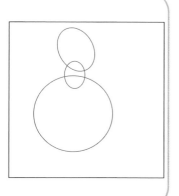

4

Use the guides to help fill in the details. Draw lines for her hair. Draw her ear, nose, neck, and part of her shoulders and gown.

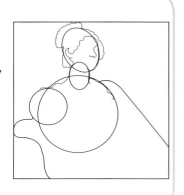

5

Draw more lines and shapes for the arms and cloak and the curved line for the back of the chair. Take your time with the hands and gloves.

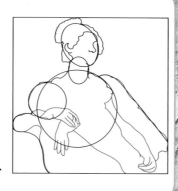

6 Erase the guides. Draw her eyes and mouth, her necklace, and the ruffle on her gown. Draw the sleeve, her glove, and the folds in her gown. Draw a line on her hat and two lines on the chair.

7

Draw the lines around her eyes, and under her mouth, nose, and neck. Draw the folds in her gown, her cloak, and on the glove she is holding. Draw two squiggly lines on her head.

8

Finish your drawing by adding shading. Start by shading lightly on her face and body, then go back and darken the shading in her hair and on her gown and cloak. Good job!

Diplomatic Career

John Quincy Adams's first diplomatic appointment came in 1794, when President George Washington sent Adams to the Dutch capital at The Hague to serve as ambassador to the Netherlands. It was the same post his father had held 14 years earlier.

In 1797, he was ambassador to Prussia. Then in 1809, President James Madison made him the ambassador to Russia. Adams was in Russia when the War of 1812 broke out. It was the second war between the United States and Britain. In 1814, Adams led peace talks in Ghent, Belgium, with the British. The agreement that was reached at the peace talks was called the Treaty of Ghent. It was a great diplomatic success for Adams. This document box, shown above, held the Treaty of Ghent. Following the peace talks, Adams served as ambassador to Britain. By this time he was considered by many to be America's most experienced and capable diplomat.

1

(blank rectangle image)

Begin by drawing a long rectangle. This will be your guide for drawing the box that held the Treaty of Ghent.

2

Draw the outline of the chest that held the Treaty of Ghent. Notice where the lines curve at the sides and the edges of the box.

3

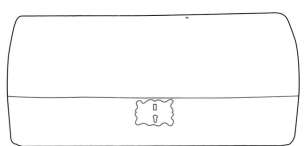

Erase the rectangle. Draw a horizontal line across the front of the chest. Then draw the brass plate on the front lower half of the chest. Be sure to add the shapes for the keyholes!

4

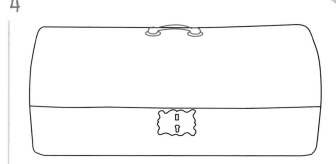

At the top of the chest, draw the shapes for the handle. See how it curves above the top of the chest.

5

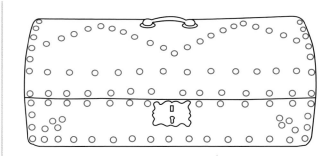

Erase the line where the handle crossed over the top of the chest. Add the circles to the chest. Try to match the pattern in the picture.

6

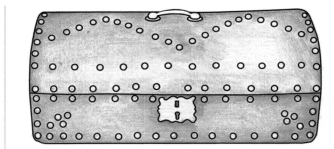

Finish your drawing with shading. Shade the circles decorating the chest lighter than the rest of the box to make them stand out more. Shade the handle lighter, too.

Secretary of State

John Quincy Adams became secretary of state under President James Monroe in 1817. He served in that role for eight years until he was elected president. While serving as secretary of state,

Mississippi River

Territory gained through Transcontinental Treaty

U.S. territory before 1819

Spanish territory

Adams negotiated the Transcontinental Treaty with Spain. Also called the Adams-Onis Treaty, this famous deal convinced Spain to give Florida and the Oregon Territory in the West to the United States. This meant that the U.S. borders now extended all the way to the Pacific Ocean. The orange areas mark the territory gained through the Transcontinental Treaty.

Adams made history again when he helped create the Monroe Doctrine, which warned European nations against claiming American land. This doctrine helped the United States take one step closer to becoming an independent nation with the power to stand up to the rest of the world.

1

Start the map of the United States by drawing a rectangle.

2

Next draw a rough outline shape for the United States from the West Coast to the East Coast. Look carefully at the drawing and copy the shape.

3

Within the guideline you drew in step 2 of the United States, go back and draw squiggly lines on the inside. Draw the shapes at the top for the Great Lakes.

4

Erase the guides. Then begin drawing the borders on the states along the East Coast, which is on the right side of the map, by following the picture.

5

Once you have drawn the states along the East Coast, keep going with the states in the middle, as shown here. The western edge is the Mississippi River.

6

Draw the long squiggly line dividing the western territories.

7

Draw a thick line in the top left corner. The line should go from the line you drew in step 6 to the West Coast.

8

Shade in the different parts of the map. The bottom left part should be darkest, and the top left and bottom right should be a little lighter. Leave the other parts unshaded.

The Election of 1824

John Quincy Adams ran for president in 1824 against three men. They were Henry Clay, William H. Crawford, and Andrew Jackson. Most people voted for Jackson. To win the election, however, a candidate needs a majority of electoral

votes, which none of them had. Electoral votes are the votes that represent what the majority of people within each state want. When no candidate won the majority of electoral votes, the House of Representatives voted among the top three candidates. They were Crawford, Jackson, and Adams. Clay was no longer a candidate, but he was Speaker of the House of Representatives. When Clay decided to support Adams, that secured the election for him.

Many people were angry about the outcome of the election. This crock, or large pot, was created to protest Adams's victory. The writing on the crock reads "25,000 majority Gnl Jackson."

1

Begin your drawing with a rectangle. You will draw the crock within this shape.

2

Draw the outline of the crock inside the rectangle. Note where the crock curves in near the top. Draw a curved line beneath this area. Leave a small space in the line. Add another curved line at the very top of the crock.

3

Erase the rectangular guide. Draw the thin oval at the top for the crock's opening. Look carefully at the drawing and draw the lines for the ship. Also draw a short line at the top, where the crock curves in.

4

Draw the lines in the ship's sails and in the flag flying from the ship. Notice how the lines slant in different directions in the different parts of the sails.

5

Draw the cracks and chips on the crock. Then write in the text under the ship. It reads, "25,000 MAJORITY GNL JACKSON." Andrew Jackson was a general in the War of 1812. He became famous for beating the British in the Battle of New Orleans.

6

Finish the crock by shading it in. If you shade it darker on the bottom and sides, it will make the image look more rounded. Nice work!

A Challenging Presidency

Andrew Jackson's supporters did all they could to spoil Adams's presidency. In fact his years in the White House proved to be the low point of John Quincy Adams's career. During his one term as president, Adams pushed for the federal government to have more power than the states. He wanted to build roads and canals that would make travel easier. Adams also wanted to create a national university and an observatory to study the stars. However, many of his ideas were turned down by Congress.

One of the biggest challenges Adams faced as president was a tariff, or a tax, charged on foreign goods brought into the country. In 1828, he signed a bill that introduced the highest tariff rates America had seen. People were so angry about it that the law became known as the tariff of abominations. An abomination is something hated. Adams lost the election in 1828 to Andrew Jackson.

1

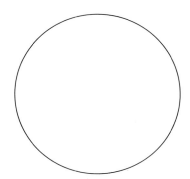

Begin by drawing a circle. This will help you draw the John Quincy Adams medal. The medal was created in 1825, the year John Quincy Adams took office as president.

2

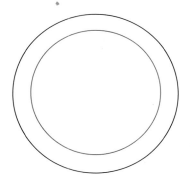

Draw another circle within the first circle. This will help you position your drawing of the side view of Adams on the coin.

3

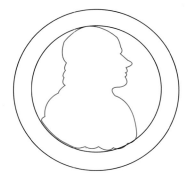

Draw the outline of the head, the neck, and the shoulders. Make sure to draw a short bumpy line at the bottom.

4

Erase the inner circle you drew in step 3. Draw another circle just inside the circle you drew in step 1. Draw the shape for his ear. Then draw the lines for his hair. Draw his eye, the side of his nose, and his lips. Draw lines to make his coat and a button.

5

Fill in the rest of the details on his face and his coat. Write "JOHN QUINCY ADAMS PRESIDENT OF THE UNITED STATES" and "1825" around the edge of the medal.

6

Finish the drawing of the medal with shading. Good work!

Adams Opposes Slavery

In 1830, John Quincy Adams became the first president to serve in Congress after leaving the White House. He was a

member of Congress for 17 years. He became most famous during that time as an antislavery leader. His arguments against slavery were so powerful that Adams earned the nickname "Old Man Eloquent." An eloquent person speaks effectively or powerfully.

In 1838, Adams argued against Texas entering the Union. If Texas became a state, it would mean adding another state where slavery would be allowed. In 1841, Adams argued before the U.S. Supreme Court for African prisoners who were charged with murder. The prisoners had taken over a Spanish slave ship called the *Amistad*. They had been forced from Africa and were going to become slaves in Cuba. Adams convinced the Supreme Court to set the men free.

1

You are now going to draw the *Amistad*. Begin by drawing a rectangle.

2

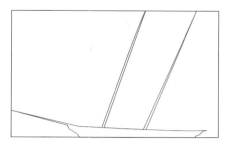

Draw the bottom of the ship and the two poles. Make sure the front of the ship comes to a sharp point.

3

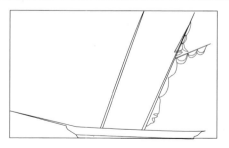

Start drawing the details on the back pole. Draw a short slanted line on the bottom of the boat.

4

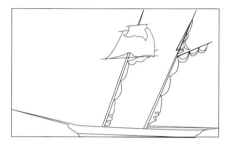

Draw details on the front pole. It has two open sails on it. Add lines to the back of the boat.

5

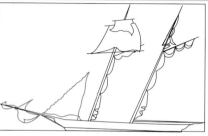

On the front of the ship, draw the sail and the ropes along the bottom.

6

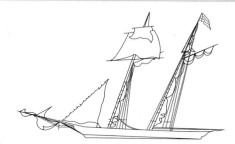

Erase the rectangle. Add ropes. Draw the small flag on top of the back pole. Add small lines to the front sail and to both poles.

7

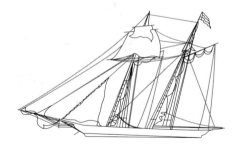

Following the drawing carefully, draw many lines connecting different parts of the ship together. These are more ropes.

8

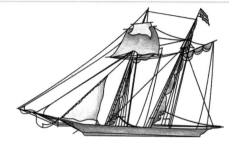

Finish the drawing with shading. Shade the bottom of the boat darkest. Shade the large top sail lightly. Then shade the small sails.

At Home in the House

No public office ever gave Adams so much pleasure as being a member of the U.S. House of Representatives. While in Congress, his dream of advancing

scientific knowledge was finally realized when the Smithsonian Institution, the large museum and research center in Washington, D.C., was founded in 1846. Adams was elected chairman of the congressional committee in charge of establishing the Smithsonian.

In 1846, Adams opposed the Mexican War because he thought it was only being fought so that the United States could gain more territory where slavery would be allowed. Two years later, while voting against giving medals to generals of the Mexican War, Adams suffered a stroke. He died two days later at the Capitol, where the House of Representatives meets, on February 23, 1848. Adams was 80 years old. Above is an 1814 drawing of the Capitol while it was under construction.

1

Begin by drawing a long rectangle. This will be your guide to drawing the U.S. Capitol, which was under construction in this image.

2

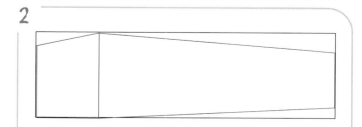

Draw the vertical line that is the corner of the building. Draw two sloping rectangles to make two sides of the Capitol.

3

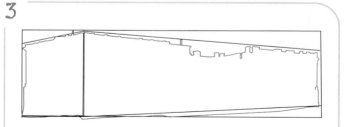

Draw the detailed outline of the Capitol building in and around the sloping rectangles, as shown.

4

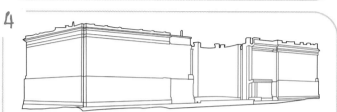

Erase the guides. Draw horizontal lines and shapes along the top, middle, and bottom. Then add all the vertical lines and shapes.

5

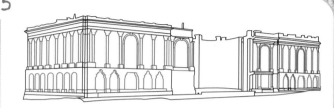

Draw the columns and the archways. Draw the columns first and try to space them out evenly across the front and the side of the building. Then add the archways.

6

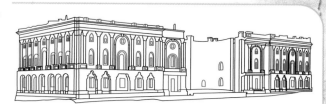

Draw the small windows and doors throughout the Capitol. Add the details to the inside of the windows. Draw the small rectangles inside the base of each column. Add details to the roof and the chimneys.

7

Draw the horizontal lines along the bottom half of the Capitol, as shown. Add small vertical lines at the very bottom.

8

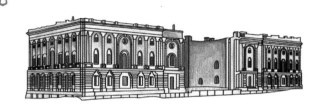

Finish your drawing of the Capitol by shading it in. Be sure to shade the inside of the windows and doors the darkest. Look at the picture closely.

Ahead of His Time

John Quincy Adams loved his country and worked hard to help all Americans. Although his manner was usually gruff and unfriendly, Adams was known for speaking the truth. He fought for what he believed in, no matter how many people opposed him. Adams's  diplomatic skills helped make peace with Europe and gained valuable territory for the United States. He defended human rights and freedom of speech in the U.S. House of Representatives. He also forced America to talk about its most serious problem of the time, which was slavery. His fierce antislavery speeches later inspired Abraham Lincoln's Emancipation Proclamation, which freed slaves in 1863. Although Adams made quite a few enemies during his lifetime, when he died in 1848 the country came together to honor him as a man who always put his country first.

1 Begin this picture of John Quincy Adams by drawing a rectangle. Draw two ovals inside the rectangle, one for the upper body and one for the head of the president.

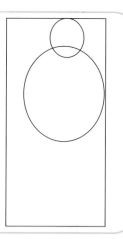

2 In this step, draw two stretched-out ovals for his legs, and two small circles for his feet. Notice how the stretched-out ovals cross over each other and are positioned on the left.

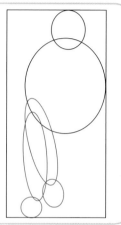

3 Begin a detailed outline of the head, shoulders, legs, and feet. Then draw the arms and hands in the upper body. Now draw his backside.

4 Erase the body guides. Add details to the head, the face, and the hand. Then draw the collar on his coat. Draw the handkerchief in his hand, the bottom of his coat, and the crease in his pant leg.

5 Draw the outline of the chair he is sitting in, starting with the arms of the chair and working your way down to the legs.

6 Draw the final details in John Quincy Adams's face, ear, and neck. Then draw the buttons on his coat, and other details on his clothing and shoes, as shown.

7 Draw the details in the arms of the chair. Draw lines for the bars of the chair behind his legs.

8 Finish your drawing with shading. Notice how the shading is darker in some areas than in others. Adams was the first president ever photographed. He is about 80 years old in this picture.

Timeline

1767	John Quincy Adams is born in Braintree, Massachusetts, on July 11.
1778	Adams travels to France with his father to attend schools in Europe.
1782	Adams travels to St. Petersburg, Russia, as secretary to Francis Dana.
1785	Adams returns to America.
1786	Adams attends Harvard College. He graduates the following year.
1790	Adams begins his career as a lawyer.
1794	Adams is appointed American ambassador to the Netherlands.
1797	Adams marries Louisa Catherine Johnson. His father, John Adams, is elected second U.S. president and names John Quincy ambassador to Prussia.
1802	Adams is elected to the Massachusetts State Senate.
1803	Adams serves as a U.S. senator from Massachusetts until 1808.
1809	Adams is appointed American ambassador to Russia.
1814	Adams negotiates the Treaty of Ghent, ending the War of 1812.
1815	Adams is appointed American ambassador to Great Britain.
1817	Adams serves as secretary of state under James Monroe.
1818	Adams negotiates the Four Point Treaty with Great Britain.
1819	Adams negotiates the Transcontinental (Adams-Onis) Treaty with Spain.
1823	Adams helps write the Monroe Doctrine.
1825	Adams is elected the sixth president of the United States.
1828	Adams loses the election to Andrew Jackson.
1830	Adams is elected to the U.S. House of Representatives, and he serves there until his death.
1836	Congress approves a rule to prevent the discussion of slavery.
1844	That rule is overturned due to Adams's efforts.
1848	John Quincy Adams dies in the Capitol on February 23.

Glossary

admired (ad-MYRD) Respected or looked up to.

ambassador (am-BA-suh-der) An official representative of one country who visits another country or who represents his or her country to organizations, such as the United Nations.

American Revolution (uh-MER-uh-ken reh-vuh-LOO-shun) Battles that soldiers from the colonies fought against Britain for freedom, from 1775 to 1783.

antislavery (an-tee-SLAY-vuh-ree) Having to do with working to end slavery.

Continental Congress (kon-tih-NEN-tul KON-gres) A political body that directed the American Revolution.

Declaration of Independence (deh-kluh-RAY-shun UV in-duh-PEN-dints) An official announcement signed on July 4, 1776, in which American colonists stated they were free of British rule.

diplomatic (dih-pluh-MA-tik) Having to do with handling relations between one's country and other countries.

document (DOK-yoo-ment) A written or printed statement that gives official information about something.

electoral (eh-lek-TOR-ul) Relating to an election.

Emancipation Proclamation (ih-man-sih-PAY-shun prak-luh-MAY-shun) A paper, signed by Abraham Lincoln during the Civil War, that freed all slaves held in Southern territory.

foreign (FOR-in) Outside one's own country.

medals (MEH-dulz) Small, round pieces of metal that are given as a prize.

negotiation (ni-GOH-shee-ay-shun) A discussion to try to reach an agreement.

observatory (ub-ZUR-vuh-tor-ee) A building in which scientists study the stars and the weather.

politics (PAH-lih-tiks) The science of governments and elections.

stroke (STROHK) A sudden weakness or sickness caused by a blockage of blood in the brain.

transcontinental (trans-kahn-ti-NEN-tul) Something that goes across a continent.

triumphs (TRY-umfs) Great successes.

tutors (TOO-terz) Teachers who who give private lessons, often in a special subject.

volunteered (vah-lun-TEERD) Gave one's time without pay.

Index

Web Sites

Due to the changing nature of Internet links, PowerKids Press has developed an online list of Web sites related to the subject of this book. This site is updated regularly. Please use this link to access the list:

www.powerkidslinks.com/kgdpusa/jqadams/